D0394522

Marie Curie

By Lisa Wade McCormick

Reading Consultant
Cecilia Minden-Cupp, PhD
Former Director of the Language and Literacy Program
Harvard Graduate School of Education
Cambridge, Massachusetts

Children's Press®
A Division of Scholastic Inc.
New York Toronto London Auckland Sydney
Me

Designer: Herman Adler Design
Photo Researcher: Caroline Anderson
The photo on the cover shows Marie Curie.

Library of Congress Cataloging-in-Publication Data

McCormick, Lisa Wade, 1961–
 Marie Curie / by Lisa Wade McCormick.
   p. cm. — (Rookie Biographies)
 Includes index.
 ISBN 0-516-25040-X (lib. bdg.)   0-516-21445-4 (pbk.)
 1. Curie, Marie, 1867–1934—Juvenile literature. 2. Women chemists—
Poland—Biography—Juvenile literature. 3. Women chemists—France—
Biography—Juvenile literature. 4. Chemists—Poland—Biography—Juvenile
literature. 5. Chemists—France—Biography—Juvenile literature. I. Title.
II. Rookie biography.
 QD22.C8M38 2006
 540'.92—dc22   2005021746

CHILDREN'S PRESS, and ROOKIE BIOGRAPHIES®, and associated
logos are trademarks and/or registered trademarks of Scholastic Library
Publishing. SCHOLASTIC and associated logos are trademarks and/or
registered trademarks of Scholastic Inc.
1 2 3 4 5 6 7 8 9 10 R 15 14 13 12 11 10 09 08 07 06

Do you wonder how things work?
Marie Curie did.

4

Marie Curie was a famous scientist. Her work helped doctors treat cancer and other illnesses.

Curie was born Maria Sklodowska in 1867 in Warsaw, Poland. She would not change her name to Marie for many years. Her nickname was Manya.

Young Maria (third from left) with her sisters and brother

8

Maria was a good student.
She started college in 1891.
Maria attended the Sorbonne,
a famous school in Paris, France.
She graduated in three years with
degrees in physics and math.

Maria changed the spelling of
her first name when she was in
France. *Marie* is how you would
say "Maria" in French.

Marie met Pierre Curie in 1894. He was a scientist, too. Pierre and Marie got married in 1895. They had two daughters, Irene and Eve.

Marie and Pierre dedicated their lives to science. They often worked so hard they forgot to eat.

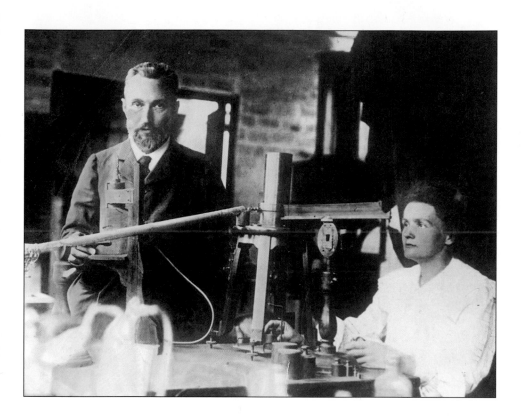

Pierre and Marie Curie (left) showing another scientist how radium glows.

In 1898, the Curies discovered two new elements. An element is matter that is made up of only one kind of atom.

Atoms make up everything on Earth. An element cannot be broken down into a simpler substance because it is made of only one kind of atom.

Marie called one element polonium after her homeland, Poland. She called the second element radium. It glowed in the dark. It also radiated, or gave off, heat.

Marie invented a word for elements with these glowing rays. She called them radioactive.

Other elements such as uranium are also radioactive. But radium is much more powerful than uranium. Over time, doctors learned to use radium to treat people with cancer.

Elements such as uranium (above) are also radioactive.

Radium is so powerful that it can also be harmful. Marie and Pierre sometimes got sick from working around this element so much.

The Curies won the Nobel Prize in Physics (above) in 1903.

In 1903, the Curies won the Nobel Prize in Physics. The Nobel Prize is the world's top award in science.

The Curies received this award for their work with radioactive elements. Marie was the first woman to win a Nobel Prize.

Marie's life was not always easy.
Pierre died in 1906 when a
horse-drawn carriage ran
him over.

Marie kept working hard after
Pierre died. She kept studying
the mysterious glowing rays.

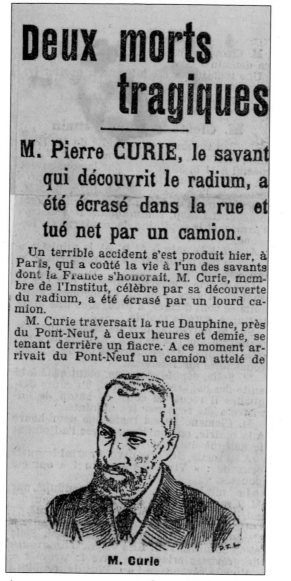

Deux morts tragiques

M. Pierre CURIE, le savant qui découvrit le radium, a été écrasé dans la rue et tué net par un camion.

Un terrible accident s'est produit hier, à Paris, qui a coûté la vie à l'un des savants dont la France s'honorait. M. Curie, membre de l'Institut, célèbre par sa découverte du radium, a été écrasé par un lourd camion.

M. Curie traversait la rue Dauphine, près du Pont-Neuf, à deux heures et demie, se tenant derrière un fiacre. A ce moment arrivait du Pont-Neuf un camion attelé de

M. Curie

A newspaper report from 1906 about Pierre Curie's death

19

Marie Curie (seated, second from right) at a meeting with other scientists in 1911

Marie won the Nobel Prize in Chemistry in 1911. She got this award for discovering polonium and radium.

Marie was the first person to win two Nobel Prizes. She earned the respect of scientists around the world.

Marie believed that it was important for scientists to keep studying radium. In 1914, she opened the Radium Institute in France. It's now called the Curie Institute.

23

An X-ray machine used during World War I

Marie's work changed the world. X-ray machines were invented because of her discoveries.

X-ray machines involve a stream of light that is able to pass through solid objects. Doctors use X-ray machines to see inside bones, teeth, and other body parts.

Many lives were saved during World War I (1914–1918) because of Marie's work. Doctors used X-ray machines to help treat wounded soldiers.

Marie's health suffered because of her work with radium. She died in 1934.

Marie's daughter, Irene Joliet-Curie, continued her mother's studies. Irene won a Nobel Prize in 1935 for her work with radioactivity.

Marie and Irene are the only mother and daughter to have each won a Nobel Prize.

Marie Curie (left) and her daughter Irene Joliet-Curie

People will always be grateful for Marie Curie's scientific discoveries. Her work still helps sick people today.

Words You Know

Curie Institute

Marie Curie

Nobel Prize

Pierre Curie

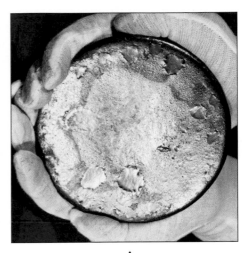

uranium

X-ray machine

Index

atoms, 12–13
birth, 6
cancer, 5, 14
college, 9
Curie Institute, 22
Curie, Pierre (husband), 10, 12, 15, 17, 18
death, 26
doctors, 5, 14, 25
elements, 12, 13–15, 17
France, 9, 22
health, 15, 26
illnesses, 5, 29
Joliet-Curie, Irene (daughter), 26
marriage, 10
matter, 12
name, 6, 9

nickname, 6
Nobel Prize, 17, 21, 26
Paris, France, 9
Poland, 6, 13
polonium, 13, 21
radioactivity, 14, 17, 26
radium, 13–15, 21, 22, 26
Radium Institute, 22
school, 9
scientists, 5, 10, 21, 22
Sklodowska, Maria, 6
Sorbonne, 9
uranium, 14
Warsaw, Poland, 6
World War I, 25
X-ray machines, 24–25

About the Author

Lisa Wade McCormick is an award-winning writer. She lives in Kansas City, Missouri, with her husband, Dave, and their two children, Wade and Madison.

Photo Credits

Photographs © 2006: ACJC-Curie and Joliot Curie Archives: 7, 8, 16, 19, 30 bottom; akg-Images, London: 11, 31 top left; Corbis Images: 3, 4, 23, 30 top (Bettmann), 28 (Hulton-Deutsch Collection), 15, 31 top right; Getty Images/Roger Viollet: 27; Library of Congress: cover; Mary Evans Picture Library: 12; Science Museum/Science & Society Picture Library: 20; The Image Works/Science Museum/SSPL: 24, 31 bottom.